PRINCE

PURPLE REIGN

'The only person who knows anything about my music . . . is me.'

– Prince

PRINCE
PURPLE REIGN

Illustrations by **Coco Balderrama**

Text by **A.D. Hitchin**

Plexus, London

1977

'What many people do not know is that Prince had his own rules even as a young person. Regardless, he did what he wanted to do and when he wanted to do it . . . He would sit and listen to the radio and play the songs he heard.'
– Sharon Nelson, Prince's half-sister

'He could hear music even from a very early age. When he was three or four, we'd go to the department store and he'd jump on the organ, any type of instrument there was. Mostly the piano and organ. I'd have to hunt for him, and that's where he'd be – in the music department.'
– Mattie Shaw, Prince's mother

'[Before Prince became famous] He was [. . .] what we would call an urban legend in the Minneapolis area, you know there were these hushed conversations about this sixteen-year-old kid who was the next Stevie Wonder, and played all these multiple instruments.'
– Dez Dickerson,
Prince's lead guitarist 1978-82

'Chris Moon came over and played me the demo tape, and being a musician myself . . . my musician antenna went up . . . I said, "Hey this group is pretty good, who are they?" And he said, "It's just one kid, just turned eighteen, and he's singing and playing and writing everything."'
– Owen Husney, the manager who signed Prince's first contract to Warner Bros

'We had this knock down drag out fight, that lasted about 3 months over his name, and his name, as you know, is Prince Rogers Nelson. I was working at an ad agency and I said, "Look, you know Prince, you can't beat that name, that's the ultimate name for a new pop rock star". And Prince said, "No, no that's not the name I want". So if he had had his way, and got his name, today we would not be mourning the loss of Prince, we'd be mourning the loss of Mr. Nelson.'
– Chris Moon (producer who discovered a young Prince) on Prince's name

1980

'We had morphed into the Spandex kids. We were trying to dress as outrageously and outlandishly as we could. We were doing two shows at the Roxy in LA. Between shows, [manager] Bob Cavallo came back and went through his list of critiques. For Prince, it was, "You're wearing these Spandex pants with no underwear. It's obscene." When Bob left, Prince got that look on his face. He said, "Bob wanted me to wear underwear, so I'll wear underwear." So he went out in his underwear. Period."

– Dez Dickerson, guitarist for Prince and the Revolution

1981

"We get on stage and within two minutes of the first song the audience, which was a hardcore hippie crowd, they took one look at Prince and went what the heck is this? And they started booing, flipping us the bird . . . And they're throwing whatever they could get their hands on . . . a crumpled up Coca-Cola can. I saw a fifth of Jack Daniels whiz by Prince's face."

– Matt Fink, keyboardist for Prince and the Revolution

1982

" From the very early days, we were controversial. We were black and white, we were girls and boys, and we were traveling together. We'd go to truck stops in Bible Belt country, and people would look at us like they wanted to kill us. But we were like brothers and sisters. We loved each other. "

– Lisa Coleman, keyboardist and guitarist for Prince and the Revolution

1985

" The reason I didn't use musicians a lot of the time had to do with the hours that I worked. I swear to God it's not out of boldness when I say this, but there's not a person around who can stay awake as long as I can. Music is what keeps me awake. There will be times when I've been working in the studio for twenty hours and I'll be falling asleep in the chair, but I'll still be able to tell the engineer what cut I want to make. I use engineers in shifts a lot of the time because when I start something, I like to go all the way through. There are very few musicians who will stay awake that long. "

– Prince

1987

" We go to the studio. We were in there for three days, almost four days straight. When he's finished, I go into the studio and I'm listening to the music. I asked him on the way home: "Did you have all that in your head? Not just the lyrics, not just the music, not just the melodies, but the arrangement, everything?" And he said, "Yeah, you know, I have to get it out when it's in there, or I can't sleep." He had written [the first two sides of] *Sign O' the*

Times. He had basically written an album in a three-and-a half-hour plane ride. 🟉
– Gilbert Davison, Prince's manager

🟉Sequencing a record with him was really extraordinary. He put so much value in the sequence. Each side was like an act in a play: it had to have a beginning, middle and an end. Great artists understand that a work of art should give you a sense of momentum when you first encounter it, and a sense of momentum when you walk away from it. 🟉
– Susan Rogers, sound engineer

1989

🟉He did it how he wanted to do it, but it never appeared arrogant, to me anyway. He seemed to have this beautiful, cool, elusive image. And it seemed real. And, if he did use it to market himself, he did that better than anyone else, too. 🟉
– Michael Keaton, lead actor in Tim Burton's *Batman*

1990

🟉Anyone who was around back then knew what was happening, I was working. When they were sleeping, I was jamming. When they woke up,

I had another groove. I'm as insane that way now as I was back then. 🟉
– Prince

1991

🟉 The only person who knows anything about my music . . . is me. 🟉
– Prince

🟉[Warner Bros.'] urban department didn't think there was a song on the album that they could get played on radio. So I get him on the phone, and he said, "Maybe I could take so-and-so and turn it around." Then he stopped and said, "It's a marketing problem. You guys deal with it." And he hung up. That was on a Friday. On Monday, I get a call from him, and he says, "You've got yourself a new baby." It was an amazing new track, "Gett Off." It turned out to be a big hit. 🟉
– Lenny Waronker

🟉His whole idea was of a band as a gang, that we were gonna go kick some ass. "We want people to be scared when they see our equipment." During the Purple Rain Tour, the Revolution would go out to clubs in their stage clothes, and we did that, too. He loved to go where another band was playing and take over.

That's the closest thing he's got to a family, or friends. "

– Tommy Barbarella

1992

" He didn't seem human. Sometimes he would just appear. You don't even know he's in the building, and the next thing he's standing right next to you. You think, "Where the hell did he come from?" "

– Michael B. Nelson, trombone player and horns arranger for Prince and the New Power Generation

1993

" He didn't want [the symbol] to be perfect. Like a human body, it's asymmetrical, imperfect. Lastly, the symbol also evokes a cross. It's impossible to know the depths of Prince's intentions, but the Love Symbol swiftly harmonizes ideas often in conflict– man vs woman, sex vs religion. "

– Mitch Monson, creative designer

" I flew to Paisley Park the day after he decided his name was now a symbol. I walked in to the receptionist, and I said, "I need to talk to him." The usual protocol was to page him. She said, "We haven't figured this whole thing out." I said, "How do you get in touch with him?" She said, "We just wait 'til we see him in the halls, and we run and grab him." "

– Jeff Katz (photographer)

1994

" In the future, I might be interactive. You might be able to access me and tell me what to play. "

– Prince

" He genuinely was hurt. He didn't know that he didn't own his own stuff. It was just lack of communication with his managers and lawyers, whether they didn't tell him or he didn't want to know. He felt like his songs were his children and someone took his children from him. He really changed then. At that point, he took control. He started signing the checks, literally. "

– Tom Tucker, music producer and recording engineer

" I followed the advice of my spirit. I'm not the son of Nell. I don't know who that is — "Nell's son" — and that's my last name . . . I would wake up nights thinking, "Who am I? What am I?" "

– Prince

1995

❛ This is what my record company has reduced Prince to. So now Prince is dead. They've killed him. ❜

– Prince, explaining "slave"

1996

❛ Our dispute was not the content but the quantity. He had artistic control. We didn't want to stifle his creative spirit. ❜

– Bob Merlis (Warner Bros Senior Vice President) to *USA Today*, on the dispute between WB and Prince

1998

❛ I sold out Wembley Stadium in a day once. So when I heard that I said, "Then put another day on sale." And they [his advisors at the time] said, "No, you don't want to do that. It might be half full." So? I'd play a half-full stadium. ❜

– Prince

1999

❛ It's not only his ability to play so many instruments, it's the level at which he plays them. I've heard him play piano like Chick Corea or Herbie Hancock, move over to bass and play like Larry Graham, then play guitar like Jimi Hendrix or Buddy Guy. ❜

– Sheryl Crow on the Artist, who plays virtually all the instruments on *Rave*.

❛ We were doing *Emancipation*, and he had a cuss jar. He was getting into Jehovah's Witnesses. He was trying to quit cussing himself. George Benson, who's a full-fledged Jehovah's Witness guy, was at Paisley doing a record. He said, "I don't know about our boy. I don't think our boy's going to make it." He couldn't get past the part of Prince cussing and trying to get religious after doing a song like "Sexy MF." No one knew what Prince was doing. This was right after Mayte lost the baby. ❜

– Ricky Peterson

❛ Now I know other men I can see how in time [Prince] is with women. It's the way he notices every detail about you . . . and when he looks at you he makes you feel like you're the center of the universe. That's very beguiling. ❜

– Mayte on Prince several years after their divorce.

2000

' A big change happened for me in the year 2000 . . . Once I changed my name back and the war was finished with my so-called enemies, I started reading the Bible intensely, and I came to find out that this is . . . this is the truth. '
– Prince

2005

' The *One Nite Alone* Tour was one of the nicest gigs I'd done with him. It was mostly new music, and it was a pretty wide-open affair. Prince really seemed to enjoy himself. It seemed to me he came to terms with the fact that he's not going to be selling 15,000-seat arenas anymore. He seemed to think, "Now I've got a good band, and I can just go out and play music for music's sake." '
– Eric Leeds

2007

' Prince gave up on the industry a decade ago. He's made his millions so all he cares about now is getting his music out to as many people as possible.

If he could drop them out of a helicopter over London, he would do. '
– Stewart Williams
(Managing Director, *Q Magazine*)

2008

' He will continue to make great records for as long as he wants to. A man like that cannot be stopped. '
– Pharrell Williams

2015

' Like books and Black lives, albums still matter. '
– Prince

2016

' His main purpose was so he wasn't stuck in one genre. He wanted to be able to crossover, and cross racial barriers. And I think he did it well. '
– Gayle Chapman,
Prince's Keyboardist 1978-1980

REMEMBERING PRINCE

"Saddened by Prince's death. Proud to have seen in the New Year with him. He seemed fine and played brilliantly funky music."

– Sir Paul McCartney

"Step away from your computer. Walk around, blast some Prince. It's the only thing that has saved my day, it may save yours."

– Lin-Manuel Miranda

"He's somewhere within every song I've ever written. I am sad, but I will smile when I think of every second that I had the fortune of being in his company. We have lost our greatest living musician. But his music will never die."

– Justin Timberlake

"Few artists have influenced the sound and trajectory of popular music more distinctly, or touched quite so many people with their talent. As one of the most gifted and prolific musicians of our time, Prince did it all."

– Barack Obama

"I'm a man of words I'm kinda speechless on losing #Prince it's like the Earth is missing a note. Little to say – only thing to do is play . . ."

– Chuck D

'Prince was a revolutionary artist, a great musician, composer, a wonderful lyricist, a startling guitar player but most importantly, authentic in every way. Prince's talent was limitless. He was one of the most unique and talented artists of the last 30 years.'

– Mick Jagger

'I'm so sad about the death of Prince, he was a true genius, and a huge inspiration for me, in a very real way.'

– Eric Clapton

'This is truly devastating news. The greatest performer I have ever seen. A true genius. Musically way ahead of any of us.'

– Elton John

'He was such an inspiration. Playful and mind-blowingly gifted. He was the most inventive and extraordinary live act I've seen. The world has lost someone truly magical. Goodnight dear Prince.'

– Kate Bush

'Goodbye sweet Prince. Pure, certified genius at the highest level. Too soon.'

– Pete Townshend

'He was a great musician. He loved music, he loved playing his instrument, and, you know the times that we did jam together were amazing, with all the various people he would bring together. And most of all, he brought all the various cultures together, he could play classical music if he wanted to, he could play jazz if he wanted to, he could play country if he wanted to. He played rock, he played blues, he played pop, he played everything. He was just a great musician, and very cognizant of what his responsibility was as a musician and a human being.'

– Stevie Wonder

❝I never saw a huge difference between the private person and the public persona with Prince. I saw one person. When you were with him he could be serious or he could be incredibly funny and goofy, which is the side I always liked because we used to laugh and talk.❞

– Lenny Kravitz

❝He changed the world!! A true visionary. What a loss. I'm devastated. This is not a love song.❞

– Madonna

❝What a genius, we were so blessed and fortunate to have him with us. I hope that he and Bowie are in heaven talking about starting a band.❞

– Moby

❝I'm shocked to hear that Prince passed at such a young age. Musically, he could do it all: sing, play, arrange and produce.❞

– Brian Wilson

❝If there was anyone I thought would be playing when he was 80 or 85, it was gonna be Prince [. . .] People know him from the ways he looked, and the different ways he looked, and different things he said – a lot of incredible things to remember him by. But I gotta tell you [. . .] Prince was probably the greatest guitar player we've ever seen.❞

– Eddie Vedder

❝The several times we were fortunate enough to work with him were always times of incredible showmanship and artistic brilliance, and for my money, he was one of the greatest guitarists in the world. His opening number with Beyoncé on the Grammy Awards has always been thought of as one of our greatest Grammy moments.❞

– Ken Ehrlich, executive producer of the Grammy Awards

'There was a mystique about him that made you want to know a little more about him [. . .] a very, very unique musical individual who was so into his music. He was music to the max.'

– Aretha Franklin

'I'm not even gonna say Rest In Peace because it's bigger than death. I never met the man (I was too nervous the one time I saw him) and I never saw him play live, regrettably. I only know the legends I've heard from folks and what I've heard and seen from his deep catalog of propellant, fearless, virtuosic work. My assessment is that he learned early on how little value to assign to someone else's opinion of you [. . .] A vanguard and genius by every metric I know of who affected many in a way that will outrun oblivion for a long while. I'm proud to be a Prince fan (stan) for life.'

– Frank Ocean

'I felt a great kinship with Prince. And he was a guy, when I'd go to see him, I'd say, "Oh, man, OK, back to the drawing board." There was a film of him on the Arsenio Hall show, where he plays a series of songs in a row. It's just some of the greatest showmanship I've ever seen. And he knew everything. He knew all about it, and then could put it to work. Just since the Sixties and Seventies and your Sam and Daves and your James Browns, he's one of the greatest showmen to come along. I studied that stuff a lot and put as much of it to use as I can with my talents. But he just took it to another level.'

– Bruce Springsteen

'He embodied a change in our culture, that in retrospect was inevitable, but he was riding that wave before a lot of us recognised it coming.'

– Alan Leeds, Prince's Tour manager 1983-1989 & President of Paisley Park Records 1989-1992

FOR YOU

' My father was so hard on me. I was never good enough.
It was almost like the Army when it came to music . . .
I wasn't allowed to play the piano when he was there because
I wasn't as good as him. So when he left, I was determined to get
as good as him, and I taught myself how to play music. And I just
stuck with it, and I did it all the time. And sooner or later, people in the
neighborhood heard about me and they started to talk. '

– Prince

'With love, sincerity and deepest care, my life with U I share.' So begins the opening track on Prince's 1977 debut *For You*, and it's a sentiment that would last a lifetime. Though little on *For You* hinted at the eclectic, genre-bending genius to follow, it did establish Prince as a one-man-band. The cover sported the now ubiquitous legend 'Produced, Arranged, Composed and Performed by Prince', with the young Minneapolis wunderkind reportedly playing all twenty-seven instruments. Prince's 1979 self-titled follow-up further established his reputation and provided two R&B hits: 'I Wanna Be Your Lover' and 'Why You Wanna Treat Me So Bad'. 'I Feel For You' was destined to be a hit for soul chanteuse Chaka Khan in 1984, a year the whole world would turn purple.

' I took one piano and two guitar lessons while I was in school. I wasn't really a model student. I didn't want to play the funky stuff music teachers used and I couldn't read music. It would always end up that the teacher would go through his thing, and I'd end up doing mine. Eventually they just gave me an A and sent me on my way. '

– Prince

I REALLY GET A DIRTY MIND

'When I brought it to the record company, it shocked a lot of people. But they didn't ask me to go back and change anything, and I'm real grateful. Anyway, I wasn't being deliberately provocative. I was being deliberately *me*.'

– Prince

Prince and his band spent nine weeks in the spring of 1980 opening for Rick James. The result was not only a legendary rivalry but the impetus for a new album, sound and image, that band member and guitarist Dez Dickerson said 'scared [Warner Bros] to death'. Wearing bikini briefs, high-heeled boots and a trench coat, armed

'I have a lot of creative control. They let me produce my own records, write my own songs, pick arrangements and all that. They're really open. I just do the album, give it to them, and they put it out.'

– Prince

'The *Dirty Mind* album was a critical success, but the fans weren't quite ready for it. It was R&B, new wave, punk, funk and rock all mish-mashed together. It was so innovative and different, it threw people for a loop.'

– Matt Fink, keyboardist for Prince and the Revolution

with a post-punk/new wave sound and hyper-sexual paeans to oral sex ('Head') and incest ('Sister'), *Dirty Mind* saw Warner Bros' soul star morphing into a curious mash-up of Stevie Wonder and Johnny Rotten. If it was Prince's first clash with the moral majority, it was also the real opening salvo of a career that would continue to defy boundaries, genres and expectations.

AM I BLACK OR WHITE?

> ❝ I never grew up in one
> particular culture. ❞
> – Prince

❝ I❜m sure wearing underwear and a trench coat didn't help matters, but if you throw trash at anybody, it's because you weren't trained right at home', said Prince to the *Los Angeles Times*, regarding the now infamous aggression and hostility displayed towards him and his band as the opening act for the Rolling Stones 1981 *Tattoo You* tour. Rather than buckle under the vitriolic backlash and barely repressed suggestions of racism and homophobia, Prince instead crafted *Controversy*, a statement of defiance and revolt that became one of the most important album releases of 1981. It was also the year Prince wrote and produced the first self-titled album by The Time, a band that would become one of his most enduring and successful creations.

> ❝ People would say something
> about our clothes or the way we
> looked or who we were with, and
> we'd end up fighting. I was a very
> good fighter. I never lost. I don't
> know if I fight fair, but I go for it. ❞
> – Prince

The Controversy
Love Thy
Neighbo

The Controversy
Annie Chris
Sentenced to

I WAS DREAMIN'
WHEN I WROTE THIS . . .

‘ What's missing from pop music is danger. There's no excitement and mystery – people sneaking out and going to these forbidden concerts by Elvis Presley or Jimi Hendrix. ’

– Prince

‘Don't worry, I won't hurt U, I only want U to have some fun’ announces the robotic voice at the beginning of ‘1999’, Prince's ultimate apocalyptic anthem, released in 1982 at the height of cold war paranoia. If nuclear annihilation was inevitable, Prince seemed determined to party defiantly with a visionary double album that broke Prince into the mainstream, both in the US and internationally. The irresistible chorus of ‘Little Red Corvette’ not only gave Prince his first US Top Ten hit, but also became one of the first music videos by an African-American artist to be played on MTV. The *1999* album was later listed as one of *Slant* magazine's ‘fifty most essential pop albums’ and inducted into the Grammy Hall of Fame in 2008.

‘ Sex is something we can all understand. It's limitless but I try to make the songs so they can be viewed in different ways. I know some people will go right through those [message] elements in a song, but there are some who won't. If you make it too easy, you lose the point. Most music today is too easy. People just come out and do the same old same olds over and over . . . All people care about nowadays is getting paid so they try to do just what the audience wants them to do. I'd rather give people what they need rather than just what they want. ’

– Prince

1982

I ONLY WANT TO SEE U

> In some ways *Purple Rain* scared me. It's my albatross and it'll be hanging around my neck as long as I'm making music.
>
> – Prince

I f the *1999* album had made Prince a star, it was *Purple Rain* that would transform him into a supernova, with a hit movie, tour and album that would go on to sell over 25 million copies worldwide and establish Prince as both an international icon and a household name. From the hyperactive stadium rock of 'Let's Go Crazy', the bass-less, hauntingly plaintive 'When Doves Cry', to 'The Beautiful Ones' soaring balladry, the album is loaded with hits and perennial Prince classics. Though the words 'and the Revolution' could be seen printed backwards on the *1999* album cover, it was *Purple Rain* that formally introduced them to the world and also a new, more inclusive working atmosphere for Prince. 'We

> 'Purple Rain' was the song Prince and the Revolution were born to record. Each member of the band added just enough of themselves to make it whole, all pushed to the edge of what music can do to a soul with one of the most iconic guitar solos in history.
>
> – Bobby Z, drummer for Prince and the Revolution

> Two pop hits doesn't mean you're a movie star . . .
> But I don't know how you describe his obsession.
> It was beyond confidence.
> It wasn't even arrogant.
> It was destiny, and either you're on board or you're going to miss out.
>
> – Alan Leeds, Prince's tour manager from 1983–1989

were a very tight unit at the time', says the Revolution's Lisa Coleman on the making of the title track. 'Each person had a specific role in the production of his or her part. It was like dancing together.' The result was nothing short of majestic: a country-gospel-rock'n'roll-soul beast; a pure outpouring of love, loss and transcendence that became Prince's ultimate signature anthem and united fans and critics in a state of delirious agreement that would never be repeated in quite the same way thereafter.

❛ He said something about having to "jack up" the story of his father in *Purple Rain* [the movie]. In truth, he said, his father didn't swear at his mother or have a gun . . . His father did kick him out of the house . . . I asked him why he was such a control freak. He said, "What if everyone left me and there was no one around except me? I'd gotta know how to control things on my own."❜

– Neal Karlen,
music writer for
Rolling Stone

'Anything I can't do?
Yeah. I can't cook.'

– Prince

'Prince was a genius with arrangements and expert at adding counter melodies, rhythms or harmony . . . 'When Doves Cry' lost its bass the moment Prince realized that the drums, lead synth and vocals were carrying the track nicely without it.'
– Susan Rogers, sound engineer

1984

THERE IS A PARK THAT IS KNOWN

Released only two weeks after the finale of the *Purple Rain* tour in April 1985, there is one thing that *Around the World in a Day* is decidedly not – a sequel to the album that had become a pop phenomenon and brought him worldwide megastardom. Prince once said he made the album to jettison the millions who bought *Purple Rain* but were not genuinely fans. And while Prince may have succeeded in mystifying many with the multi-layered, neo-psychedelia of *Around the World in a Day*, he also firmly cemented himself as one of the most truly unpredictable and virtuoso musicians in popular music. 'My hunch is that Prince conceived of the album . . . because he wanted to experiment stylistically', says

❛ In some ways, [*Purple Rain*] was more detrimental than good. People's perception of me changed after that, and it pigeonholed me. I saw kids coming to concerts who screamed just because that's where the audience screamed in the movie. That's why I did *Around the World in a Day*, to totally change that. ❜
– Prince

❛ The cover art came about because I thought people were tired of looking at me. Who wants another picture of him? I would only want so many pictures of my woman, then I would want the real thing . . . I don't mind [the album being called psychedelic], because that was the only period in recent history that delivered songs and colors. Led Zeppelin, for example, would make you feel differently on each song. ❜
– Prince

engineer Susan Rogers. '*Purple Rain* represented a new point in his commercial success and so its follow-up needed to promote a new direction if longevity was the goal.' It was also the first album to introduce the idea of his utopian playground, Paisley Park, a vision which would become a reality when Prince's recording complex of the same name was completed in 1988.

I JUST WANT YOUR EXTRA TIME AND YOUR . . .

❛ The thing is that when you're called, you're called. I hear things in my sleep; I walk around and go to the bathroom and try to brush my teeth and all of the sudden the toothbrush starts vibrating! That's a groove, you know. ❜

– Prince

Prince began recording his next album, *Parade*, by laying down the drum parts for its first four songs in a single take. And even if *Under the Cherry Moon* flopped at the cinema, the breathtaking soundtrack reeled in listeners. Propelled by the minimalist funk of 'Kiss' (famously offered to Prince's protégé group Mazarati, but reclaimed when Prince decided it was 'too good' to lose) the remainder of *Parade* dazzles with a sinuous trip through orchestrated jazz and continental-flavored funk. Originally recorded on 21 April 1985, thirty-one years to the day before Prince's own passing, the album's standout is arguably 'Sometimes it Snows in April', a yearning, elegiac folk ballad of mortality and loss that has since become Prince's unintended eulogy.

❛ The song 'Kiss' came about totally accidentally . . . I talked to one of the people at Warner Brothers on the phone, and they said, "Oh no, we're not putting that out. We don't like it [. . .] It sounds like a demo, there's no bass, there's no reverb." Luckily enough he was successful and he had enough power at the time to say, "You put that out first, or I'm not giving another single." And a year later, they were only trying to sign things to sound like it. So, that tells you where the music is supposed to come from. ❜

– David Z, sound engineer and music producer

'Prince gave us this straight version [of 'Kiss'] with just one verse, an acoustic guitar and voice, no rhythm. It was almost a folk song. We went back in the studio and stayed up all night doing this thing. In the morning, I came back around 9:30. Prince had been there, listened to what we did and put his lead guitar and voice on it. He said, "It was too good for you guys. I'm taking it back."'

– David Z, sound engineer and music producer

IN FRANCE A SKINNY MAN DIED . . .

❛ What people were saying about *Sign O' the Times* was, "There are some great songs on it, and there are some experiments on it." I hate the word "experiment" – it sounds like something you didn't finish. Well, they have to understand that's the way to have a double record and make it interesting. ❜
– Prince

Having disbanded the Revolution following the final date of the *Parade* tour in 1986, Prince returned in March 1987 with a one-man-band recording that would become one of his most influential, groundbreaking masterpieces. Fusing pop, rock, funk and R&B into a genuinely new (and oft-imitated) sound, the sprawling double LP finds Prince at the height of his creative powers. Encompassing some of the greatest articulations of all Prince's many musical personas, *Sign O' the Times* also introduces Camille, an androgynous alter ego with pitched-up helium vocals. Social concerns preoccupy the bleak syncopation of the title track, but are always balanced with optimism and hope, perhaps no more so than on 'The Cross', a bravely fervent declaration of faith and redemption. Prince chose not to appear in the music video for the title track, instead releasing one of the earliest known lyric videos. *Sign O' the Times* was voted best album of 1987 by Pazz & Jop critics poll and best album of all time by *Time Out* magazine.

❛Onstage, he broke his *Purple Rain* guitar intentionally. Me and Lisa looked at each other and went, "It's over." He disappeared . . . We had dinner, and he said: "I can't expect you guys to go where I'm going to go next. I think we've gone as far as we can go. I've got to let you go." The two of us were like, "What?" He called Bobby [Z] that night, too. We were all completely spun out. We thought we'd be around a lot longer. We were ready to be there.❜
– Wendy Melvoin, guitarist for Prince and the Revolution

LOVESEXY IS THE ONE
'TIL MY DAY IS DONE

❛ I was very angry a lot of the time back then, and that was reflected
in that album [*The Black Album*]. I suddenly realized that we can die at
any moment, and we'd be judged by the last thing we left behind.
I didn't want that angry, bitter thing to be the last thing. I learned
from that album, but I don't want to go back. ❜

– Prince

'DON'T BUY THE BLACK ALBUM. I'M SORRY' reads the hidden message in the video for Prince's 'Alphabet St', an apology for the album he abandoned at the eleventh hour following a spiritual epiphany. Whether or not the decision was influenced by a rumored bad trip on ecstasy, it represented a pivotal moment in Prince's career. Though Prince recalled all copies, a hundred European promo editions of *The Black Album* remained in circulation and were widely bootlegged. Fans were now aware of the treasure trove of unreleased recordings in Prince's vault, leading to an explosion in the trade of bootleg recordings. The album itself was eventually begrudgingly released by Prince in 1994 as a means of fulfilling his contractually obliged albums to Warner Bros and finds Prince in blistering form, responding to criticisms that

❛ [*Lovesexy* is] a mind trip, like a psychedelic movie. Either you went with it and had a mind-blowing experience or you didn't. All that album cover was, was a picture. If you looked at that picture and some ill came out of your mouth, then that's what you are – it's looking right back at you in the mirror. ❜

– Prince

he had lost touch with his black roots with a dark slab of pure molten funk. The shocking scenario of domestic abuse played out on 'Bob George' saw Prince heading into new territory, pitch-shifting his voice into a deep octave to portray a violent, paranoid partner in a song that's been remarked as an early prototype of gangsta rap. Only the sensually delicate 'When 2 R in Love' survived to live another day on *Lovesexy*, the album Prince chose to release instead, a single mind-melding forty-five-minute track of spiritual rebirth and liberation. Although *Lovesexy* is considered by many to be Prince's gospel album, it was still beset by controversy for its cover, picturing a nude picture of our hero, that provoked some record stores to wrap the album in . . . *black*.

❛ That's what I went through with *The Black Album*. All this gangsta rap, I did that years ago. 'Cause if you're gonna do something, go all the way in. ❜
– Prince

❛ I was an expert at cutting off people in my life and disappearing without a glance back, never to return. Half the things people were writing about me were true. ❜
– Prince

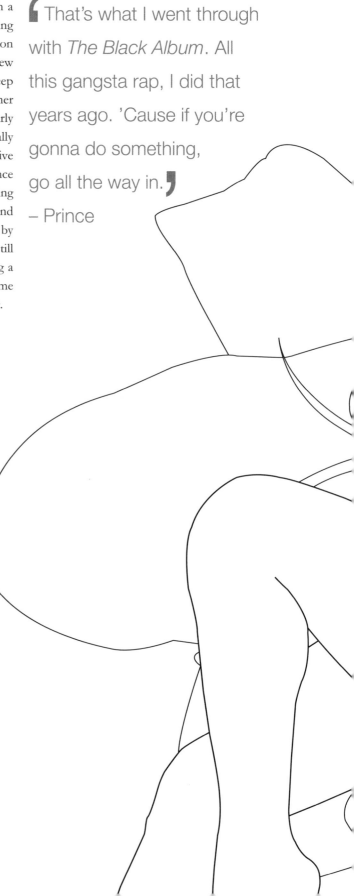

I'VE SEEN THE FUTURE AND IT WILL BE . . .

In December 1988 director Tim Burton called Prince and asked if he would rerecord two of his songs he had used in the rough cut of his forthcoming *Batman* movie. The result was a collection of entirely new Prince songs inspired by the film that became both a soundtrack as well as Prince's eleventh studio album. Attributing lyrics to characters from the movie, as though he is singing on their behalf, *Batman* is determinedly a *Prince* album rather than a movie-tie in, with Prince using the theme of dualities presented in the film to explore his own psychology of light

❛You know how the very first song I learned to play was 'Batman'? There are no accidents. And if there are, it's up to us to look at them as something else. And that bravery is what creates new flowers.❜

– Prince

❛There was so much pressure on Tim. For the whole picture, I just said, "Yes, Mr Burton, what would you like?"❜

– Prince

versus dark, good versus evil. Film critic Matt Zoller Seitz praised Prince's *Batman* songs and music videos as 'more psychologically perceptive than any of the Batman films.' The album represented a commercial revival for Prince, claiming the Number One spot on the *Billboard* albums chart for six consecutive weeks. It has since gone on to sell over eleven million copies.

❛I brought Prince over to London and you could just tell his kind of genius was in touch with the movie. By the time we had dinner that night, he had three songs in his head. Three weeks later, he had nine songs.❜

– Mark Canton,
Batman film producer

THERE ARE THIEVES IN THE TEMPLE TONIGHT

❝There's nothing a critic can tell me that I can learn from. If they were musicians, maybe. But I hate reading about what some guy sitting at a desk thinks about me. You know, "He's back, and he's black", or, "He's back, and he's bad". Whew! Now, on Graffiti Bridge, they're saying I'm back and more traditional. Well, 'Thieves in the Temple' and 'Tick, Tick, Bang' don't sound like nothing I've ever done before.❞

– Prince

Despite being publicized as a sequel movie to *Purple Rain*, with Prince reprising his role as 'The Kid' and his legendary rivalry with Morris Day and The Time, *Graffiti Bridge* bombed both critically and at the box office. Prince later reflected that 'maybe it will take people thirty years to get it' and it's likely that the film's spiritual message was simply too out of step with mainstream audiences in 1990. Happily, the album was much better received with pop's Picasso

❝ People are going, "Oh, this is Prince's big gamble." What gamble? I made a $7 million movie [*Graffiti Bridge*] with somebody else's money, and I'm sitting here finishing it.❞

– Prince

❝I feel good most of the time, and I like to express that by writing from joy. I still do write from anger sometimes, like 'Thieves in the Temple'. But I don't like to. It's not a place to live.❞

– Prince

delivering a sprawling complex soundtrack with enough melodic appeal to balance his eclectic experimentalism. While 'Thieves in the Temple' was that summer's big hit, it was 'The Question of U' and 'Joy in Repetition' that became bona fide Prince classics and were frequently performed live by Prince for the rest of his career.

1990

IF I GAVE U DIAMONDS AND PEARLS

❝I make music because if I don't, I'd die. I record because it's in my blood. I hear sounds all the time. It's almost a curse: to know you can always make something new.❞

– Prince

At the 1991 MTV Video Music Awards, Prince delivered a timeless example of what swagger truly *is*. Wearing a now infamous buttocks-exposing yellow suit, he delivered a Caligula-style performance of 'Gett Off', his new hip-hop heavy funk jam with the recently inaugurated New Power Generation. Keen for a return as a commercial force, Prince turned his attentions to crafting new music with a new band that would reference

❝I like music to play in my car, and when I need something new to play I record something. Instead of buying a tape, I make music.❞

– Prince

❝You know when you buy someone's record and there's always an element missing? The voice is wrong or the drums are lame or something? On mine there's nothing missing.❞

– Prince

current trends without conforming or sacrificing his artistry. The result was *Diamonds and Pearls*, a bestselling album that produced a slew of hit singles and propelled Prince to his popular zenith in Europe. 'Cream' (reportedly written by Prince while staring at himself in the mirror) became Prince's fifth and final US Number One single.

'I've already made
money, all the money
I need. I was never
that interested in money
anyway. '
– Prince

MY NAME IS PRINCE AND I AM FUNKY

First introduced to the world on the bestselling *Diamonds and Pearls*, it was a year later on 1992's *Love Symbol* album that the New Power Generation came to full flower. With an album cover bearing the golden glyph that would later become Prince's name, proceedings nevertheless begin with the funk/rap bombast of 'My Name is Prince' before expertly veering through an array of stylistic transitions ably abetted by the NPG's master musicianship, running the gamut of R&B, jazz, reggae, hip-hop, rock and pop (often in the space of a single song) and some of Prince's meanest dance cuts since *The Black Album*. Prince reaches his spiritual peak on the album's biggest hit, '7', the video for which showed Prince symbolically killing previous incarnations of himself.

❝ Don't come to the concert. I've got a band of assassins. ❞
– Prince

❝ The NPG wasn't a collective by any means, but he loved the band concept. With Michael [Bland] on drums, he had a band that could do anything musically on the drop of a dime. On *Diamonds and Pearls* and that next record [*Love Symbol*], he would come in with the tunes, pretty skeletal, and we'd try this, try that, throw out ideas. We had played together so much, we got to know what he wanted. Things would happen very fast. We cut entire records in a day sometimes. 'Sexy M.F.' was one take. ❞
– Tommy Barbarella, keyboardist for Prince and the New Power Generation

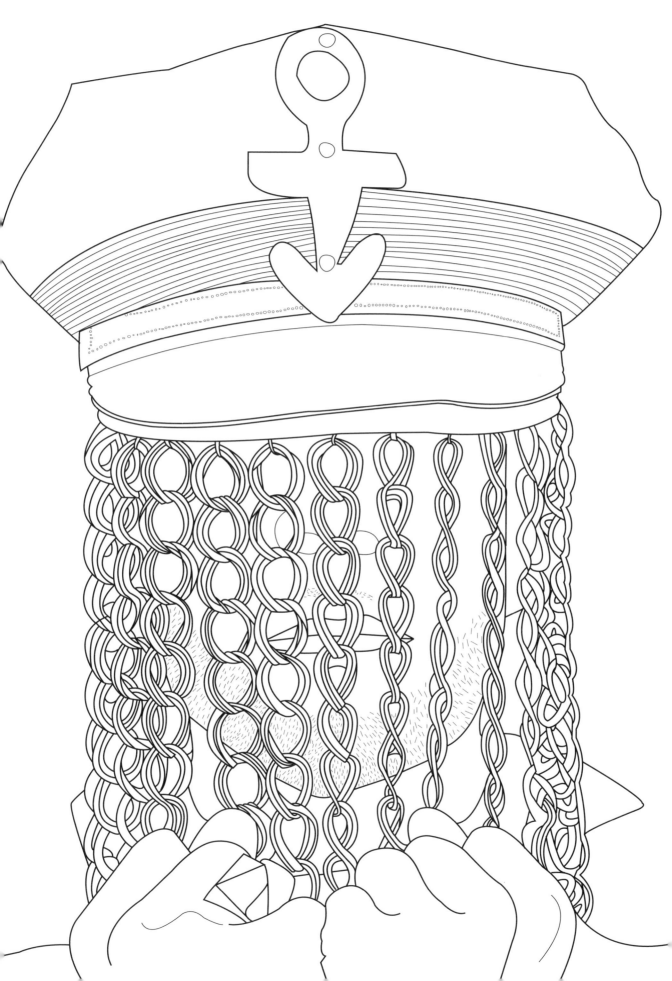

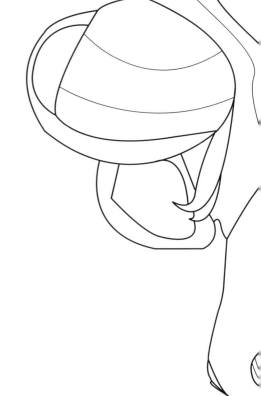

> Warner Bros took the name, trademarked it, and used it as the main marketing tool to promote all of the music I wrote. The company owns the name Prince and all related music marketed under Prince. I became merely a pawn used to produce more money for Warner Bros.
>
> – Prince

'It is an unpronounceable symbol whose meaning has not been identified. It's all about thinking in new ways, tuning in 2 a new free-quency', Prince wrote in a public statement announcing his name change on June 7 1993, a move that both shocked and mystified the world. Mitch Monson, creative designer for this latest incarnation of the symbol (it had appeared in a simpler, prototype variation much earlier in Prince's career, most notably on the *Purple Rain* album cover), said, 'He really wanted to see this feminine quality to [the symbol], and have this mix of male and female. He saw those elements being important, and being integrated.' Integrated or not, the symbol caused problems for Warner Bros, who couldn't say or even type their star's new name, leading the media to refer to Prince as 'The Artist Formerly Known As Prince' (TAFKAP) or simply 'The Artist'. More than anything, the name change symbolized a break from Warner Bros, who Prince felt were trying to rein in his output with fears he would saturate the market. Warner Bros released *The Hits/The B-Sides* in September 1993, having paid Prince not to be involved in the production process. The set included a live version of Prince's 'Nothing Compares 2 U', originally released by protégé group The Family on their 1985 self-titled LP, and made a worldwide hit by Sinéad O'Connor in 1990.

1993

COULD U BE THE MOST BEAUTIFUL GIRL IN THE WORLD?

Challenged by a Warner Bros executive that he could never make another hit, Prince crafted 'The Most Beautiful Girl in the World', a dreamy ballad that became a worldwide chart success and Prince's only Number One single under any name in the UK. The consent given Prince by Warner Bros boss Mo Ostin to release the single independently was, however, a one-off deal and despite (or in spite of) his success Prince soon found himself at loggerheads with Warner Bros again. Later that year, Prince delivered two albums – *Come* (credited to Prince) and *The Gold Experience* (credited to Symbol) – asking Warner Bros to release both simultaneously. Warner Bros, fearing saturation of the market, opted to release *Come* only, the cover of which bore

> **But I'm not bitter. I'm not angry. Mo Ostin (Warner Bros boss) gave me 'The Most Beautiful Girl in the World' to release as Symbol. And I will love that man forever because of that.**
> **– Prince**

> **Imagine yourself sitting in a room with the biggest of the big in the recording industry, and you have "slave" written on your face. That changes the entire conversation.**
> **– Prince**

the legend 'Prince: 1958–1993', marking the album as a posthumous release by his former identity. Prince meanwhile, derided the *Come* album as 'old', choosing instead to perform and promote the more commercial songs featured on the unreleased *Gold Experience*. As part of this protest, Prince wrote 'SLAVE' on his face, seeking the liberation of his master recordings and release from the ills of the corporate contract he felt was hampering his artistic destiny.

1994

ALL THAT GLITTERS AIN'T GOLD

❛ I got a whole new mindset when I became Symbol. I can't explain how I feel now compared to then. I don't want to destroy the mystique by revealing everything. And if people come to see me just to hear 'Purple Rain' then I'm sorry. I'm playing these songs now. I'll play Prince songs occasionally. I just want people to understand who I am. ❜

– Prince

Though fans rejoiced when *The Gold Experience* was finally released in September 1995, it failed to meet commercial expectations. Overshadowed by Prince's very public dispute with Warner Bros, Prince's initial, very successful promotions for the album a year earlier had lost momentum, and Prince, having toured the album extensively from 1994–95, appeared to have lost interest. Even though *The Gold Experience*'s golden hour may have passed, it still contained some truly brilliant material and was a success with critics, many of whom considered it his strongest, most cohesive record in years. Of the two singles, 'I Hate U', a courtroom drama about a cheating woman, was rumored to be dedicated to former protégée Carmen Electra, while 'Gold', a rousing anthem considered by Prince to be 'the next "Purple Rain"', was a Top Ten hit in the UK.

❛ I don't care. If people think I'm insane, fine. I want people to think I'm insane. But I'm in control. It was different before I became this. I didn't have control. I didn't know what was happening beyond the next two albums. But now I know exactly what the next two albums will be. I'm not playing anyone else's game. I'm in control. I don't care if people say I'm mad. It don't matter. ❜

– Prince

WE SHOULD ALL COME 2GETHER 2 THE NEWPOWER SOUL

'If you don't own your masters, your masters own you. Underline that. The more people you allow to come between you and your music, the further it moves away from you. This isn't your business, it's your life.'

– Prince

Joyously liberated from his recording contract with Warner Bros in November 1996, the purple floodgates opened with Prince releasing the celebratory thirty-six-song, three-disc opus *Emancipation* a week later, followed by *Crystal Ball*, a five-disc set of unreleased rarities and previously bootlegged tracks in January 1998. Fired up creatively and relishing his newfound creative freedom, Prince began writing and producing albums for Chaka Khan and former Sly & the Family Stone bassist Larry Graham for release on his NPG label, both of whom appeared on *Newpower Soul*, his next summer release of 1998. Unlike the two previous albums credited to the New Power Generation (1993's *Gold Nigga* and 1994's *Exodus* respectively), *Newpower Soul* features lead vocals from Prince on every track in addition to his usual writing and production duties. Despite some lukewarm reviews bemoaning the album's preoccupation with partying and funk jams, 'Come On', 'The One' and 'Wasted Kisses' were three deeper, mostly overlooked cuts that have since remained firm fan favorites. It was also during this period that Prince first began studying the Bible with Larry Graham (an Elder of Jehovah's Witnesses), an experience that reportedly led to a religious conversion and would influence his outlook markedly in the coming years.

' I think it's a landmark record for me. I allowed other sounds made by other individuals . . . The New Power Generation is like a studio, like an idea. It's a way of doing things.'

– Prince

RAVE UN2 THE JOY FANTASTIC, RAVE!

'Dreams are real life; real life is the dream.'

– Prince

1999 found Prince not so much partying, but working with Arista records mogul Clive Davis on a one-album deal that sought to remodel Santana's star-studded *Supernatural* album success as his own commercial revitalization. Crediting 'Prince' as a producer, the Artist returned to the title track of his unreleased 1988 album, engaging guest stars Gwen Stefani, Sheryl Crow, Chuck D, Eve, Ani DiFranco and Maceo Parker to craft a pop and R&B album with chart appeal. Although *Rave* was certified gold by the Recording Industry of America and peaked at Number Five in the Canadian charts, it failed to connect with audiences elsewhere. Following pay-per-view event *Rave Un2 the Year 2000*, featuring Prince's threatened last performance of '1999', and Arista's cancellation of two further singles, Prince created the NPG Music Club to deliver his music directly to fans, becoming one of the first artists to ever use the Internet as his own distribution outlet. Although Prince reverted to his given name after his publishing contract with Warner/Chappell expired on 16 May 2000, he continued to use his now iconic logo on album art, clothing and in concert appearances.

'Bass is primal, and it reminds me
of a large posterior – but both spirituality
and sexuality originate higher up in the body.
I see them as angelic.'

– Prince

'I've got more money
than I ever had,
more gold, more land.
Do I give a damn about
the charts when I'm
making this money?'

– Prince

DON'T U WANT 2 COME? 3121

Following several years of independent releases that kept the purple faithful happy, Prince returned triumphantly to public prominence in 2004 with a legendary performance and induction into the Rock and Roll Hall of Fame. With the release of the *Musicology* album and attendant *Musicology Live 2004ever* tour, school was now in session, with Prince selling more than 1.4 million tickets in his mission 'to bring back music and live musicianship'. In 2006, Prince enjoyed his first Number One *Billboard* album since 1989's *Batman* with *3121*, a concise, focused set that harked back to his '80s accomplishments with contemporary relevance. The club

❛ Really, I'm normal. A little highly strung, maybe. But normal. But so much has been written about me and people never know what's right and what's wrong. I'd rather let them stay confused. ❜

– Prince

❛ I don't need no producer, I don't need no record company, no A&R man or anyone telling me what to do. I produce my own records in my own studio. Why do I need someone telling me what to do, and owning what I do? ❜

– Prince

banger 'Black Sweat' reminded Pharrell and Justin Timberlake exactly *where* they found the funk, shaking rumps and reinforcing Prince's renewed critical and popular success in equal measure.

❛ I don't let computers use me. It's more interesting to me to pick up a guitar and create a sound out of thin air. That's analogue. We're analogue creatures; we breathe air, we hear soundwaves, we react to spirit and color. A computer's binary. ❜

– Prince

2007

BUT NOT LIKE I LOVE MY GUITAR . . .

❝I'm not going to waste my blessings. God has over-blessed me, but you have to appreciate what you have, and to do that, you have to break down a lot of walls, meaning that you're not afraid anymore.❞

– Prince

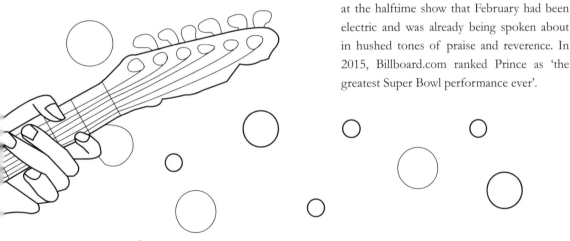

In 2007, Prince raised eyebrows once again when he announced that he would play twenty-one nights at London's O2 arena and give his new *Planet Earth* album away for free with the *Mail on Sunday*. When 600,000 extra people rushed out to buy the newspaper and Prince's O2 *Earth Tour* quickly sold out and became *the* capital's hot ticket, all doubters and critics were quickly vanquished. Remembered by the O2 as 'a mind-blowing feat', his twenty-one-night run has never been beaten since. It is not as though the sceptics had reason not to detect the full extent of his purple revival on the winds. His Super Bowl performance before 140 million viewers at the halftime show that February had been electric and was already being spoken about in hushed tones of praise and reverence. In 2015, Billboard.com ranked Prince as 'the greatest Super Bowl performance ever'.

❝ It was raining when it was time to go on –
but it wasn't raining hard enough to stop us.
The producer asked if we were okay, and Prince
was like, "Can you make it rain harder?"❞
– Morris Hayes, keyboardist, on
Prince's Super Bowl performance

ART OFFICIAL AGE IN THE FUTURE

What is a hit? All the terms those gangsters came up with for songs: hits, bullets, smashes. It's all violence. Everything they taught us is inverted.

– Prince

'These are performances by one of the greatest funk-rock bands ever', proclaimed *The Guardian* in response to Prince's historic UK hit-and-run shows with female rock trio 3RDEYEGIRL. Reunited with his classic record label Warner Bros following a new landmark deal that saw Prince finally regain ownership of his catalogue of classic recordings, both parties celebrated with the release of two new albums on the same day. *PLECTRUMELECTRUM*, Prince's debut album with 3RDEYEGIRL, saw Prince strapping on his electric guitar to dive headlong into heavy rock territory, but it was the wonder of Prince's solo brilliance on the electro-funk majesty of *Art Official Age* that captured critical acclaim, delivering a late-career classic and his strongest album in decades.

You reach a plane of creativity and inspiration. A plane where every song that has ever existed and every song that will exist in the future is right there in front of you. And you just go with it for as long as it takes. Like tonight. You can tell me I was onstage for four hours, but it doesn't feel like that to me. We were all out of body out there. Sometimes it isn't until we're in the car after a jam where I feel my leg tighten up. And then I'm not out of body anymore.

– Prince

SUCH A THING AS TIME . . .

‘No, I don't think about gone. I just think about in the future when I don't want to speak in real time.’

– Prince

Happy with a new deal with Jay-Z's streaming service Tidal, which allowed Prince the creative freedom to make his music available more freely, he surprised us again in 2016 by moving into uncharacteristically vulnerable and personal territory. Announcing an autobiography with Random House intended for release a year later, Prince's solitary *Piano and a Microphone* shows were markedly biographical and exposed with the legendarily secretive artist revealing more of himself than ever before. After being briefly hospitalized following what was to become his final show in Atlanta, Prince passed away unexpectedly a week later at his beloved Paisley Park studios on 21 April. For a moment that evening, monuments across the globe turned purple as the world mourned and celebrated one of the most extraordinarily gifted and boundary-breaking artists of his or any other generation; a symbol, an icon, more than a name.

YAMAHA

"Well, I'm not one to get bad reviews. So I'm doing [the *Piano and a Microphone* tour] to challenge myself, like tying one hand behind my back, not relying on the craft that I've known for thirty years. I won't know what songs I'm going to do when I go on stage, I really won't. I won't have to, because I won't have a band. Tempo, keys, all those things can dictate what song I'm going to play next, you know, as opposed to, "Oh, I've got to do my hit single now, I've got to play this album all the way through," or whatever."

– Prince

First published in 2018 by Plexus Publishing Limited
This edition copyright © 2018
by Plexus Publishing Limited
Published by Plexus Publishing Limited
The Studio, Hillgate Place
18-20 Balham Hill
London SW12 9ER
www.plexusbooks.com

British Library Cataloguing in Publication Data
A catalogue record for this book is available
from the British Library

ISBN-13: 978-0-85965-552-1

Book and cover design by Coco Balderrama
Illustrations by Coco Balderrama
Front cover design by Fresh Lemon
Thanks to Catherine, Joanna, Sophie and Craig at
Fresh Lemon for their initial help with the
illustrations and cover design.
Text by A.D. Hitchin
Printed in Great Britain by Bell & Bain Ltd, Glasgow

Acknowledgements

Prince and his colleagues, family and friends have given
innumerable interviews throughout his career. These
have proved invaluable in writing and researching the
book. Thanks are due to: **Books:** *Prince: Life & Times*
by Jason Draper (2017), *Prince* by Matt Thorne (2013),
Prince: An Artist's Life 1958-2016 by the Editors of *Time*
(2016), *Prince: Inside the Music and the Masks* by Ronin Ro
(2016), *Celebrating Prince: 1958-2016 Special Collector's Edition*
by *People Magazine* (2016), *Let's Go Crazy: Prince and the
Making of Purple Rain* by Alan Light (2015), *Prince: A Pop
Life* by Dave Hill (1989), *Prince: A Documentary* by Per
Nilsen (1993), *Prince: The First Decade* by Per Nilsen (2003).
Newspapers and periodicals: the *Los Angeles Times,*
*Slant, Time Out, Q, Vibe, Mojo, Billboard, Ebony, Guitar
World, Insider, New Yorker, Pitchfork,* the *Star Tribune, Vanity
Fair, Dazed, Uncut, Vogue, Variety, Rolling Stone, NME,* the
New York Times, the *Telegraph,* the *Guardian.* **Websites:**
princevault.com, pitchfork.com, housequake.com,
officialprincemusic.com, musicfeeds.com, pinknews.co.uk,
startribune.com, kstp.com, latimes.com, theguardian.
com, billboard.com, princetext.tripod.com, nme.com, npr.
org, nytimes.com, bbc.co.uk, youtube.com, twitter.com,
facebook.com, prince.org, instagram.com. **Television
and radio:** 1991 MTV Video Music Awards (MTV, 5
September 1991); *Rave Un2 the Year 2000* (In Demand,
31 December 1999), Super Bowl halftime show (CBS, 4
February 2007). **Film:** *Purple Rain* (1984*); Under the Cherry
Moon* (1986); *Sign 'o' the Times* (1987); *Batman* (1989);
Graffiti Bridge (1990).

We would like to thank the following photographers and
photographic sources for supplying the inspiration for
the illustrations: Cover; September 1991 *Spin* magazine
cover; Robert Whitman; Allen Beaulieu/NPG Records/
Warner Bros, *Dirty Mind* album cover; Allen Beaulieu/
NPG Records/Warner Bros, *Controversy* album cover;
NPG Records/Warner Bros, *1999* single cover; NPG
Records/Warner Bros; Ed Thrasher, Stuart Douglas
Watson/NPG Records/Warner Bros; The LIFE Picture
Collection/Getty Images; Jeff Katz/NPG Records/
Warner Bros, *Parade* album cover; NPG Records/Warner
Bros, *Mountains* single cover; Jeff Katz/NPG Records/
Warner Bros; Rob Verhorst/Redferns; Jean Baptiste
Mondino/NPG Records/Warner Bros, *Lovesexy* album
cover; NPG Records/Warner Bros, *Batdance* music video
single cover; Bob McNamara/NPG Records/Warner
Bros; NPG Records/Warner Bros, September 1991 *Spin*
magazine cover; Randee St. Nicholas/NPG Records/
Warner Bros, *My Name is Prince* single cover; Randee
St. Nicholas/NPG Records/Warner Bros, *The Hits/
The B-Sides* album cover; Alfred Steffen/AFP; NPG
Records/Warner Bros; Steve Parke/NPG Records; Steve
Parke/NPG Records/Arista, *Rave Un2 the Joy Fantastic*
album cover; Frank Micelotta; Jeff Haynes/AFP/Getty
Images; Kevin Winter/Getty Images; NPG Records. It
has not always been possible to trace copyright sources
and the publisher would be glad to hear from any such
unacknowledged copyright holders.